CONTENTS

Words in **bold** are explained in the glossary on page 31.

FESTIVALS
AROUND THE WORLD

WHAT IS A FESTIVAL?

A festival takes place when people in a community come together to celebrate a particular event or time of year. Festival celebrations happen for many different reasons and can take place in communities all around the world. Celebrations may last for only a single day, but others can go on for many months.

Each festival has its own set of diverse customs and traditions that form part of the celebrations. Communities can celebrate festivals in a number of ways, including taking part in religious **ceremonies**, holding large street processions and performing traditional dances.

A CHRISTIAN FESTIVAL IN GUATEMALA.

DURING THE HINDU FESTIVAL HOLI, IT IS TRADITIONAL FOR PEOPLE TO THROW COLOURED POWDER PAINT AND WATER AT ONE ANOTHER.

HARVEST FESTIVAL IS A RELIGIOUS FESTIVAL WHERE CHRISTIANS CELEBRATE THE FOOD GROWN AND HARVESTED ON FARMS.

WHY ARE FESTIVALS CELEBRATED?

Sometimes, festivals are celebrated because they are times of the year that hold religious significance. There are hundreds of different religious festivals held around the world every year.

Other festivals are celebrated because they have become part of a cultural tradition. This means that a festival began through the beliefs and practices of communities' **ancestors** being passed down over a long period of time.

Festivals can also be celebrated for both cultural and religious reasons. For example, Christmas is considered to be a religious (Christian) festival that is held to remember the birth of Jesus Christ. However, many people who do not follow Christianity still celebrate Christmas because it has become part of their cultural tradition.

CHINESE
NEW YEAR

WHAT IS CHINESE NEW YEAR?

Chinese New Year is a spring festival that is mostly celebrated in China and happens in January or February of every year. A long time ago, Chinese New Year was celebrated to worship particular gods and goddesses. Today, most people celebrate Chinese New Year as part of the cultural tradition to mark the beginning of each new year.

A TRADITIONAL DRAGON DANCE THAT IS PERFORMED DURING CHINESE NEW YEAR.

FESTIVAL FOOD

Families from all over China – as well as many other parts of the world – come together on New Year's Eve to enjoy a traditional **reunion** dinner called Nian Ye Fan. Dumplings filled with meat or vegetables, called jiaozi, are eaten after midnight. A coin is hidden in one of the jiaozi and whoever finds it is believed to have good luck and fortune for the rest of the year.

JIAOZI

GIFTS

It is a common custom during Chinese New Year for children to be given gifts of money in red envelopes called packets. Children keep these envelopes under their pillows for the seven nights after Chinese New Year ends. This is believed to bring them good luck for the rest of the year. Other gifts such as mandarin oranges, chocolate and candles are also exchanged between friends and families.

For Chinese people the colour red symbolises good luck, fortune and happiness. This is why they decorate their houses with red decorations during the festival.

THE LANTERN FESTIVAL

On the last day of the festival, a large street parade takes place called the Lantern Festival. People line the streets to enjoy the music, parades, acrobats and traditional dances that the festival has to offer.

THE LANTERN FESTIVAL

Chinese lanterns are traditionally made from oiled rice paper on a bamboo frame — although most are made from paper nowadays — and every one has a small candle inside.

THE DRAGON DANCE

The dragon dance is one of the many dances performed during the Lantern Festival. A dragon costume is held up by many performers who move its head and body so that it looks like it is dancing. The dance is performed to scare away evil spirits and to bring good luck in the new year.

HANUKKAH

WHAT IS JUDAISM?

Judaism is a religion that was founded over four thousand years ago in the Middle East. Jewish people believe in one God and their place of worship is a **synagogue**. The **Torah** sets out God's word and instructs people on how to practise their faith.

A SYNAGOGUE IN PRAGUE.

WHAT IS HANUKKAH?

Hanukkah is a festival celebrated by Jewish people for eight days in November or December of every year. Jewish people come together to celebrate a time in history when they fought to practise their own religion freely.

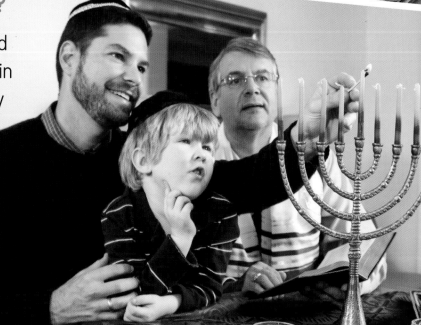

HOW IS HANUKKAH CELEBRATED?

To celebrate Hanukkah, Jewish people light eight candles on a **menorah**. A new candle is lit on every day of the eight-day festival. The flame of the candle in the middle of the menorah, called the Shamash or servant candle, is used to light the other eight candles. The light from the menorah symbolises the Jewish people's faith in God and the presence of God's light to guide them.

A Jewish Festival

SHAMASH

MENORAH

Hanukkah is also called 'Chanukah' and the 'Festival of Lights'.

PRAYER AND WORSHIP

During Hanukkah, religious ceremonies are held by a **rabbi** in a synagogue. Parts of the Torah are read aloud every day during the festival and the complete Hallel prayer is spoken at each morning service. The Hallel prayer is a prayer that is only recited on joyous occasions, usually during festival times.

Worship also takes place at home. After every meal, a prayer called Birkat Hamazon is read aloud. On special occasions, like Hanukkah, the prayer is sung aloud. The prayer thanks God for his goodness and for the food the family has been blessed with.

A FATHER HELPING HIS SON TO READ THE BIRKAT HAMAZON PRAYER ALOUD.

FESTIVAL FOOD

Food that has been fried in oil is traditionally eaten during Hanukkah. This is because when the **Maccabees** fought for their freedom many years ago, a miracle occurred; a tiny drop of oil burnt for eight whole days. The eight candles lit on the menorah during Hanukkah represent this miracle. Jewish people eat lots of fried foods during Hanukkah to commemorate this miracle, which is seen as an act of God. Often sweet foods, like sufganiyots, are also eaten. Sufganiyots are jam donuts that are fried in oil and sprinkled with icing sugar.

SUFGANIYOTS

PLAYING GAMES

One of the most popular games played during Hanukkah is the dreidel game. A dreidel is a spinning top with a letter painted on each of its sides. Children play by spinning the dreidel and guessing which letter it will fall on. Whoever guesses the letter correctly wins a pot of money or gold, which usually includes a bag of chocolate coins covered in silver and gold foil.

DREIDEL

THE LETTERS ON THE SIDES OF THE DREIDEL ARE FROM THE HEBREW ALPHABET.

EID
UL-FITR

WHAT IS ISLAM?

Islam is a religion that was founded over one thousand years ago in the Middle East. Muslims believe in one God called Allah and their place of worship is a **mosque**. The **Qur'an** contains Allah's word and instructs people on how to practise their faith.

A MOSQUE IN ISTANBUL, TURKEY.

WHAT IS EID UL-FITR?

Eid ul-Fitr is a festival celebrated by Muslims for one day of every year to mark the end of **Ramadan**. It is also called the 'Festival of the Breaking Fast' because it is a time when Muslims stop **fasting** and are allowed to eat during daytime hours once again.

WHY DO MUSLIMS CELEBRATE EID UL-FITR?

Muslims believe that it was in the month of Ramadan that Allah first passed on his word to the **prophet** Muhammad. Allah's words were then written down in the Qur'an. To show their devotion to and faith in Allah, Muslims fast for one month. When the new moon comes out Eid ul-Fitr begins and fasting stops.

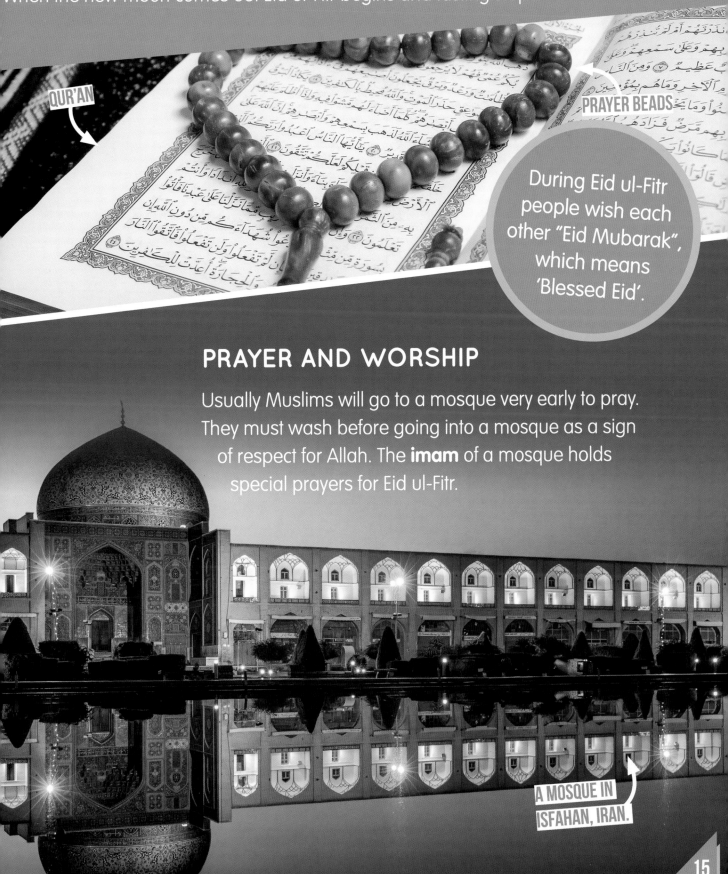

QUR'AN

PRAYER BEADS

During Eid ul-Fitr people wish each other "Eid Mubarak", which means 'Blessed Eid'.

PRAYER AND WORSHIP

Usually Muslims will go to a mosque very early to pray. They must wash before going into a mosque as a sign of respect for Allah. The **imam** of a mosque holds special prayers for Eid ul-Fitr.

A MOSQUE IN ISFAHAN, IRAN.

SHEER KORMA

FESTIVAL FOOD

Eid ul-Fitr is also known as the 'Sweet Eid' because of the amount of sweet foods eaten during the festival. A bowl of sweet milk and dates, called sheer korma, is traditionally eaten for breakfast. In the daytime, other sweet foods such as ma'amoul are eaten. Ma'amoul are small, round pastries filled with dates, figs or walnuts.

WALNUTS

MA'AMOUL

CHARITY

Eid ul-Fitr is a time to forgive others and to share with one another. Every adult Muslim who can afford to must give food to those who are poor and in need. This act is called Zakat and it is one of the **Five Pillars of Islam**. It means that everyone can celebrate this special festival together.

THE FIVE PILLARS OF ISLAM

hajj   a pilgrimage to Mecca that must be made once in a Muslim's lifetime

salat   the act of praying five times a day

sawm   fasting during the month of Ramadan

shahadah   a claim of faith and trust that there is only one true God (Allah)

zakat   giving charity to benefit the poor and needy

EASTER

WHAT IS CHRISTIANITY?

Christianity is a religion that began over two thousand years ago in the Middle East. Christians believe in one God and they pray to him in a **church**. The Christian holy book is called the Bible that includes the word of God and instructs Christians on how to practise their faith.

A CHURCH IN LONDON, ENGLAND.

WHAT IS EASTER?

Easter is a spring festival that is celebrated by Christians in March or April of every year. Christians believe that it was on Easter Sunday, many years ago, that Jesus Christ was **resurrected**. Jesus Christ is an important religious figure for Christians as they believe that he is the Son of God.

Easter is also called 'Pasch'.

WHY DO CHRISTIANS CELEBRATE EASTER?

Over two thousand years ago, Jesus Christ was nailed to a wooden cross after he had been betrayed by Judas, who was one of his twelve disciples. Jesus eventually died on the cross and was buried in a cave. Jesus came back to life three days later and remained on Earth for another forty days and forty nights. Christians celebrate the anniversary of Jesus' resurrection at Easter.

GOOD FRIDAY

The Easter festival begins with **Good Friday**. It is a time when Christians commemorate the day Jesus Christ was nailed to the cross and think about their faith in God. On this day church services are held, hymns are sung and prayers are made.

A GOOD FRIDAY CHURCH SERVICE IN STRASBOURG, FRANCE.

EASTER SUNDAY

On Easter Sunday, Christians celebrate the anniversary of Jesus Christ's resurrection. Churches are decorated with spring flowers, candles are lit and church bells are rung. After church, gifts are exchanged, traditional food is eaten and Christians celebrate their faith in God together with their families and loved ones.

MARZIPAN BALLS

A TRADITIONAL SIMNEL CAKE.

FESTIVAL FOOD

On Easter Sunday it is traditional to eat roast lamb, which is usually served at lunch or dinner. Sweet foods, such as Simnel cake, are often eaten for dessert. Simnel cake is a fruit cake that is decorated with eleven balls of marzipan to represent Jesus' 11 disciples, not counting Judas.

GIFTS AND DECORATIONS

In many countries, Easter eggs made of chocolate are given as gifts at Easter time. In other countries, such as Russia and Poland, traditional wax-covered eggs are painted with elaborate and brightly coloured patterns. Christian parents often hide these eggs all over their garden for their children to find.

EASTER EGGS AND THE EATING OF LAMB REPRESENT THE NEW LIFE THAT WAS CREATED IN JESUS' RESURRECTION.

21

DIWALI

WHAT IS HINDUISM?

Hinduism is a religion that began in India over four thousand years ago. Hindus believe in one God, called Brahman; however, they also pray to many other gods and goddesses who they believe are different forms of Brahman.

GANESH IS THE HINDU GOD OF WISDOM AND KNOWLEDGE.

The word Diwali means 'festival of lights'.

WHAT IS DIWALI?

Diwali is a festival celebrated by Hindus for around five days in October or November every year. Hindus come together to celebrate the start of the new year by exchanging gifts, setting off fireworks and decorating their homes with many lights.

WHY DO HINDUS CELEBRATE DIWALI?

During Diwali, Hindus celebrate the Goddess of wealth and **prosperity**, known as Lakshmi. They pray to Lakshmi to bring them good fortune in the new year. The festival also celebrates the return of Prince Rama and his wife, Sita, to their kingdom. Their people lit oil lamps so they could find their way home.

A DRAWING OF RAMA.

FESTIVAL OF LIGHTS

During Diwali, lamps are lit to remember Rama's faith in Brahman and a time when good won over evil. In the evening, large firework displays are held as the fireworks are thought to ward off evil spirits.

The small candles lit at Diwali are called diyas.

DIYA

RANGOLI DECORATIONS

People decorate the doorsteps of their houses and the ground outside temples with brightly coloured patterns. These are called Rangoli patterns. People make them with a mixture of rice flour, water and coloured powder. Hindus hope the Goddess Lakshmi will visit their houses when she sees the beautiful patterns and bring them wealth and prosperity in the new year.

LAKSHMI, THE HINDU GODDESS.

MANDIR

PRAYER AND WORSHIP

In the evenings, many people come together for a prayer meeting. They pray to the God Ganesh and the Goddess Lakshmi at a mandir, which is a Hindu place of worship, and give offerings of fruit and sweets in the hope that they will bring them good fortune in the new year.

MITHAI

FESTIVAL FOOD

On the fourth day of Diwali, brothers visit their sisters' houses for a traditional meal. Traditional festival foods, especially colourful sweets called Mithai, are eaten throughout the festival.

THE BIRTHDAY
OF GURU NANAK

Sikhism is the fifth largest religion in the world.

A GURDWARA IN DELHI, INDIA.

WHAT IS SIKHISM?

Sikhism is a religion that began over five hundred years ago in India. Sikhs pray to their one God in a gurdwara, which is the Sikh place of worship. Sikhs follow the teachings of their **gurus** and the **Guru Granth Sahib**, which guides them on how to practise their faith.

The celebration of Guru Nanak's birthday is also called 'Guru Nanak Gurpurab.'

WHO IS GURU NANAK?

Guru Nanak was the first of the ten gurus, who together founded the Sikh religion. Sikhs celebrate the anniversary of Guru Nanak's birthday for one day in November every year. On this day, Sikhs go to a gurdwara for prayer, hold large street processions and share a special meal together.

GURU GRANTH SAHIB

The Guru Granth Sahib contains the writings of seven Sikh gurus who lived over four hundred years ago. Copies of the book are kept in a special place in the gurdwara and are protected by a cloth **canopy**. Two days before the festival begins, Sikh men and women start to read the Guru Granth Sahib aloud from beginning to end. Each person reads for two to three hours before the next person takes over from them.

The reading of the Guru Granth Sahib all the way through is called 'Akhand Path'.

CELEBRATION PROCESSIONS

On the day before Guru Nanak's birthday, large Sikh processions, called Nagar Kirtan, are held in the streets. They are traditionally led by five people, who represent the **Five Beloved Ones** or Panj Pyare. These people dress in orange and carry the Sikh flag with them. They are followed by a procession of singers singing holy hymns and musicians playing different tunes. The procession ends with prayers at a gurdwara.

FLAG OF SIKHISM

FIVE BELOVED ONES

PRAYER AND WORSHIP

The festival starts very early in the morning, with celebrations beginning as soon as the sun rises. Sikhs travel to a gurdwara for prayer, sing hymns from the Guru Granth Sahib and share stories about Guru Nanak's life and beliefs.

KARAH PARSHAD

FESTIVAL FOOD

After prayers, a sweet food made from wheat flour, sugar and butter, known as Karah Parshad, is blessed and eaten. Everyone then shares a free meal called a langar. Only vegetarian food is served so that everyone can eat together, whether they eat meat or not.

FESTIVAL GREETINGS

Chinese New Year
Gong Hey Fat Choy
Happy New Year

Hanukkah
Hanukkah Sameach
Happy Hanukkah

Eid ul-Fitr
Eid Mubarak
Blessed Eid

Easter
¡Felices Pascuas!
Happy Easter

Diwali
Diwali Ki Shubhkamnayein
Happy Diwali

The Birthday of Guru Nanak
Happy Guru Nanak Jayanti
Happy Anniversary of Guru Nanak

GLOSSARY

ancestors	persons from whom one is descended, for example a great-grandparent
canopy	a cloth or covering held up over something
ceremonies	formal occasions celebrating achievements, people or religious or public events
church	a Christian place of worship
fasting	the act of not eating or drinking, specifically for religious reasons
Five Beloved Ones	five men who are important to the history of Sikhism because of their commitment to the Sikh faith and its teachings
Five Pillars of Islam	five actions a Muslim must complete in order to live a good and responsible life, according to Islam
Good Friday	the anniversary of the Friday that Jesus Christ was nailed to a cross
Guru Granth Sahib	the Sikh holy book
gurus	spiritual teachers in Sikhism
imam	a teacher of Islam
Maccabees	a group of Jewish people who were led by Judas Maccabaeus
menorah	a nine-branched candle-stand that is lit during Hanukkah
mosque	a Muslim place of worship
prophet	a messenger or teacher of the will of God
prosperity	success and wealth
Qur'an	the Islamic holy book
rabbi	a teacher of Judaism
Ramadan	the Islamic month when Muslims do not eat during daylight hours
resurrected	when a dead person is restored back to life
reunion	a gathering of people who have not seen each other for some time
synagogue	a Jewish place of worship
Torah	the Jewish holy book

INDEX